THE LITTLE BOOK OF CHRISTMAS AGA TIPS

RICHARD MAGGS

THE LITTLE BOOK OF CHRISTMAS AGA TIPS

RICHARD MAGGS

Absolute Press

Absolute Press
An imprint of Bloomsbury Publishing Plc

50 Bedford Square
London WC1B 3DP
UK

1385 Broadway
New York NY 10018
USA

www.bloomsbury.com
Absolute Press and the A. logo are trademarks of Bloomsbury Publishing Plc

First published in 2004.
Reprinted 2006, 2010, 2013, 2014.

A catalogue record for this book is available from the British Library.
Library of Congress Cataloguing-in-Publication data has been applied for.
ISBN 13: 9781904573203

Printed and bound in Spain by Tallers Gràfics Soler

'At Christmas an Aga excels itself. The Aga bottom oven has brought exclamations of delight from knowledgeable cooks everywhere, producing the most delectable Christmas puddings ever set alight. This handsome specimen cooked itself in our demonstration kitchens while the offices were closed and our staff in bed.'

1933 Aga brochure

1

For simple yet **stylish Christmas canapés,** serve 1-inch-sized blinis. Use 1 oz (25g) buckwheat flour, 3 oz (75g) self-raising flour, 5 fl oz (150ml) milk and an egg to make a simple batter and cook on the greased simmering plate. These can then be **topped with soured cream** and caviar or smoked salmon strips with a feather of dill.

2

To re-heat your Christmas pudding on Christmas Day, you don't need to steam it in the conventional way. Wrap the china, plastic or foil pudding basin tightly in foil and simply place **in the simmering oven** all morning, next to the turkey if necessary. Over several hours it will slowly and safely heat through, ready for serving piping hot at the end of your meal.

3

Flambé your Christmas pudding

with spectacularly sustained flames. Unmould onto a hot serving plate then warm equal quantities of cheap brandy and vodka in a pan on the simmering plate before pouring over and lighting. The secret ingredient is the vodka, which will sustain the flames dramatically for several minutes.

4

To make

Aga fudge,

place 12 oz (350g) of chopped plain chocolate with 12 oz (350g) smooth peanut butter into a Pyrex bowl in the simmering oven for 30 minutes. Stir in a 14 oz (400g) tin of sweetened condensed milk and 1 teaspoon of vanilla extract. Pour into a lined 8-inch (20cm) tin. Chill and cut 1-inch pieces. This is

quick and easy

and extremely tasty.

5

Dry your own orange slices for

Christmas wreaths and garlands.

Soak in a dilute solution of Milton first to prevent future growth of mould and then dry on wire racks on trays. Place these onto Aga chef's pads on top of the closed lids overnight. Store in an airtight tin near the Aga until needed.

(Not suitable for consumption.)

6

When making mince pies, roll out and cut the smaller lids first whilst the pastry is shortest. Save subsequent rollings for firmer disks for the bases. If making a large batch, for speed, pipe in the mincemeat using a large forcing bag without a nozzle. Bake immediately or **freeze them uncooked.** Bake on the floor of the roasting oven for 8-12 minutes, until just golden.

7

Place **mince pies**

on a plate in the simmering oven for 15 minutes before serving. This will produce delicious pies

with a gently warmed filling

that won't burn any tongues and spoil the Christmas festivities.

8

To mull wine,

combine all the ingredients from your recipe except for any spirit, and heat through on the simmering plate until just starting to steam. Cover and transfer to the simmering oven for 15 minutes. Remove, add the spirit, and allow to stand for a further five minutes before serving.

9

The large capacity of Aga ovens is **perfect for Christmas cooking.** Invest in some full size Aga baking trays for cooking large quantities of roast vegetables and trimmings. Four trays will fit in each oven at the same time. Grill bacon rolls at the top of the roasting oven, with potatoes on the floor. Swap the other trays around periodically.

10

Dry surplus cranberries in the simmering oven, and pop one tablespoon of popcorn at a time on a piece of Bake-O-Glide on the simmering plate with the lid down. Thread these up alternately using stout cotton to string up as

attractive garlands for your Christmas tree.

11

Make traditional **Christmas shortbread and gingerbread shapes** to hang on the tree with tartan ribbons. Decorate with coloured glacé icing for a festive effect to use as edible place markers for a Christmas tea. Use your favourite shortbread recipe – the best ones include a quantity of semolina or cornflour for the crispest finish.

12

Nativity salt dough sculptures are fun for children to make. Use 3 cups of plain flour with 2 cups of salt, 2 tablespoons of glycerine, 2 tablespoons of powdered wallpaper paste and $1\frac{1}{2}$ cups of water. Dry slowly in the simmering oven for several hours before painting and varnishing.

13

For attractive

frosted grapes to decorate puddings, dip bunches of two or three grapes into lightly beaten egg white, shaking off any excess, then roll in caster sugar, coating well. Place on Bake-O-Glide or baking parchment on a plain shelf in the simmering oven for 3-5 minutes until just dried.

14

Just before **filling champagne flutes,** rinse each one out with a small quantity of white wine. This will coat the glass and prevent an over-exuberant mousse overwhelming it as the fizz is poured in.

This will greatly **speed up pouring** a tray of glasses.

15

Spiced cranberry and orange compote

is easy to make. Dissolve 5 oz (125g) of granulated sugar in 8 fl oz (200ml) of orange juice. Add 8 oz (225g) of fresh cranberries and 1 rounded teaspoon of ground allspice. Cover, bring to the boil, then cook for 15 minutes in the simmering oven. Slake 1 teaspoon of arrowroot in a little cold water and stir in and cook for a minute. When cool, stir in 2 tablespoons of port.

16

Dry-fry your favourite selection of spiced nuts

for sensational home-made nibbles

– try almonds, Brazil nuts, cashews, macadamias, peanuts and pecans. Mix together with a dusting of sweet spices and caster sugar or a little curry paste and salt with a spritz of oil. Toss regularly in a non-stick tray on the floor of the roasting oven for about 8 minutes.

17

For a delicious hot sauce to serve **with Christmas pudding,** which makes a change from the usual cream varieties, try a clear ginger sauce. Chop some crystallised ginger finely, and heat through on the simmering plate with a little of the ginger syrup and some apple juice. Add a slug of ginger wine just before serving.

18

Make your own sugar plums.

Mince or process 3 oz (75g) each of currants, raisins, pitted prunes, dates and glacé cherries. Work in enough icing sugar to bind and form 1 inch (2.5cm) balls. Roll in granulated sugar and place onto baking parchment on a tray by your Aga to dry before storing in a tin.

19

To open stubbornly closed

fir cones for Christmas decorations,

give them a spell in the warming oven, or the simmering oven with the door just ajar, and they will open up, ready for spraying with gold and silver.

20

For attractive jewelled Christmas-tree biscuits, roll out and cut stars using your favourite biscuit mixture. Cut 1 inch (2.5cm) holes in the centre of each and drop in a clear, coloured boiled sweet. Use Bake-O-Glide, and as the biscuits bake the sweet will melt and set giving an attractive centre window.

21

Bread croustade cases are great for

easy canapés.

Cut out circles of thin white bread and roll thinly. Brush with melted butter and place into a bun tray with a second tray on top to press them down. Bake low down in the roasting oven for 6 minutes until crisp.

22

Forgotten to make your own mincemeat?

Doctor a bought jar, adding a grated eating apple, some grated zest and a little juice from an orange plus a generous slug of brandy. Add extra finely chopped glacé fruits and some nibbed almonds to give a really authentic finish.

23

Fry slices of **leftover Christmas pudding** in plenty of butter.

Place in an Aga baking tray and cook on the floor of the roasting oven for 5 minutes. Dredge generously with vanilla caster sugar before serving with lots of brandy butter flecked with orange zest.

24

Keep sauces hot by making brandy sauce and custard in advance, and keeping them hot in covered pans or Pyrex jugs covered with cling film in the warming or simmering ovens. Bread sauce can similarly be made early **without deteriorating.**

25

Try roasting your own chestnuts in the roasting oven. Cut an 'X' on the curved side with a sharp paring knife, place them in an Aga baking tray and sprinkle with a few teaspoons of water. Roast on the grid shelf on the floor of the oven for up to 40 minutes. You will need to enlist help to peel them while they are still warm.

26

For the most **elegant poultry carving,**

remove the wishbone before cooking. You can ask your butcher to do this for you. Alternatively, use a very sharp small knife to loosen the skin at the neck. Cut the wishbone at the base end near the wing joints first, and then cut up along the bone and twist to remove.

27

Cook a large quantity of trimmings such as chipolatas, bacon rolls or 'pigs in blankets', by threading them onto pairs of skewers. They can then be turned in one go, when needed, so that they cook evenly **with the minimum of fuss.**

28

For a perfect **Christmas continental breakfast,** place some ready-to-cook *pains au chocolat* covered with clingfilm in the refrigerator overnight. They will prove slowly, ready to bake in just 7 minutes low down in the roasting oven the following morning.

29

Get ahead by

preparing your vegetables

on Christmas Eve. Peel potatoes and keep covered with water in the refrigerator, with carrots and parsnips in polythene bags. Trim tiny Brussels sprouts, removing any discoloured leaves, then store in the refrigerator in a polythene bag containing a little water.

30

Potatoes and parsnips

can be parboiled on Christmas Eve. Shake in a colander to roughen their edges, then refrigerate in plastic bags. If you prefer, they can even be three-quarter roasted the night before, and finished off with a final half hour on the day itself. Each tray needs a spell on the floor of the roasting oven.

31

Brussels sprouts can be cooked ahead of time. Boil in salted water for 6 minutes until just cooked, then drain and refresh by plunging into iced water for 5 minutes to arrest the cooking and set their bright green colour. Drain again and chill. Re-heat in a pan with a small amount of water and a knob of butter just before serving.

32

For superlative roast potatoes

that will be the envy of experts, seek out some *Graisse d'Oie*, the best goose fat from France. If this is not available, a mixture of half vegetable shortening and half olive oil works brilliantly. Make sure each tray enjoys a spell on the floor of the roasting oven.

33

Fill your vegetable tureens with raw vegetables as you prepare them so that you can gauge the perfect quantity for the ultimate in

presentation perfection.

Heat empty tureens stacked inside themselves in the warming or simmering ovens but warm the lids on the top of the Aga so the handles remain cool enough to lift.

34

For fantastic parsnips, trim off the thin tips (which tend to burn) and save for soup and casseroles. Half-way through roasting, glaze with a little honey or brush with melted butter and dust with grated Parmesan.

35

Don't place cooked

roast potatoes

in the simmering or warming ovens – they will go soggy. Place the filled ovenproof serving dish on an Aga toaster on the floor of the roasting or baking oven, with a cold plain shelf above to

keep crisp

without over-browning.

36

Mashed or creamed carrot

with swede, squash or sweet potato is an easy dish with great colour and flavour. It keeps hot well in the warming or simmering oven and also re-heats beautifully. Add a little of the cooking liquid with some crème fraîche and season with black pepper and a little freshly grated nutmeg.

37

If steaming or baking a ham

or gammon, simmer-steam or baste using Coca-Cola. This gives a delicious depth of flavour and a particularly good colour. The finished stock may be boiled down to make an easy sticky glaze.

38

Freshly blanched almonds have much more flavour for seasonal baking and are really worth grinding yourself. Cover them in a pan with boiling water then place in the simmering oven for five minutes. Drain and the skins will slip off easily. Pat dry before grinding.

39

Make your

brandy butter weeks ahead.

Whip together 8 oz (225g) of unsalted butter, 4-6 oz (100-150g) of icing sugar and 6 tablespoons of brandy. Freeze in its serving dish and, when solid, take out and run warm water over the upturned dish. The butter will slip out in one piece for wrapping tightly in foil.

40

Make Christmas sugar mice

by sieving 12 oz (350g) of icing sugar and adding a large egg white, 3 tablespoons of glycerine and a few drops of food colouring. Gradually work in more sieved sugar to make a smooth paste. Divide and form into 8 mice with ears, adding silver balls for eyes and string for tails. Dry next to the Aga over several nights.

41

If you are **short of refrigerator space,** a car boot in December may be cold enough for the safe storage of an uncooked bird once you have taken delivery of it on Christmas Eve. Alternatively, use an unheated room or animal-proof outhouse. Use bathroom scales covered with clingfilm to weigh the stuffed bird.

42

For festive *petits fours* serve

macaroon kisses.

Whisk 2 egg whites until stiff. Add 3 oz (75g) of caster sugar by the spoonful, then 4 oz (100g) of ground almonds and $^1/_2$ teaspoon of almond essence. Pipe onto Bake-O-Glide and cook on the grid shelf on the floor of the roasting oven for 6-8 minutes, then transfer to the simmering oven for 20 minutes.

43

Giblet stock will

transform your gravy.

Cover the giblets with cold water and simmer for 5 minutes on the simmering plate, then skim. Add a clean unpeeled halved onion with a chopped carrot and a stick of celery, some parsley stalks and a few peppercorns. Bring back to the boil, cover, and transfer to the simmering oven for 3 hours.

44

For effortless basting, soak a large square of fine butter muslin generously in melted butter. Completely cover the bird with the doubled muslin, tucking the edges into the base of the tin. This will act as a wick and help prevent the turkey drying out (make sure it covers the legs well).

45

To ensure that a bird is thoroughly cooked, check that the juices run clear. If any tinge of pink shows, return to the oven. Ideally, use a meat thermometer, which should read 70-72°C (158-160°F). A further check is to 'shake hands' with the legs – they should be easy to wiggle in their sockets.

46

When making gravy, never place an Aga roasting tin on the boiling plate as over time this will cause it to distort. Cook your roux on the simmering plate or on the floor of the roasting oven. Once your hot stock has been whisked in, return there to simmer for a further 5 minutes, then season.

47

Keep your cooked bird hot

on or next to the Aga. Cover with foil then pile over several clean towels, etc., as an insulating jacket. It will keep piping hot for between 30 minutes and up to two hours, if needed. Add any juices to your gravy before serving.

48

To re-heat cold cooked turkey,

place slices in an ovenproof dish or use an Aga roasting tin. Add enough cold water to just cover the base of the container and cover tightly with foil. Place on the floor of the roasting oven for 7 minutes, until piping hot.

49

If you have a lot of plates and serving dishes to heat, with your Aga already full of food, then put your dishwasher to use. Set it to a drying or hot rinse and dry cycle. Switch on at just the right time to result in

hot, dry dishes exactly when required.

This tip never fails to impress onlookers.

50

Make a special

aromatic fire room-freshener

which will also revive an almost dead open fire. Combine satsuma peelings, apple, eucalyptus or vine trimmings and fragrant pine cones and dry in the simmering oven for several hours. Place on the fire just before guests arrive.

Richard Maggs

A dynamic and accomplished chef, Richard is an authority on Aga cookery. As well as having featured on TV and radio, he writes for several magazines and contributes a regular column to the official Aga Magazine. A bestselling author, he is also the resident Aga cookery expert, The Cookery Doctor, with the award-winning Agalinks website at www.agalinks.com.

Acknowledgements

My thanks to all my family, friends, colleagues, fellow chefs and, of course, Aga owners everywhere for their constant support and encouragement. To everyone at Aga-Rayburn; it is a pleasure to continue to work with such an enthusiastic group of people. Also, a huge thank you to my publisher, Jon Croft, and my editor and graphic designer, Matt Inwood, at Absolute Press who are now great friends and fellow Aga louts.

AGA is a registered trademark of Aga Foodservice Group plc.

Bake-O-Glide™ is a re-usable non-stick coated cooking material, available from Aga Specialists.

THE LITTLE BOOK OF
BRIDGE
TIPS
PETER FRENCH

THE LITTLE BOOK OF
CHESS
TIPS
PETER FRENCH

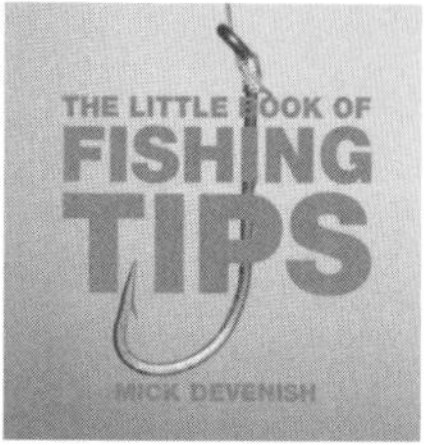
THE LITTLE BOOK OF
FISHING
TIPS
MICK DEVENISH

THE LITTLE BOOK OF
GREEN
TIPS
WILLIAM FORTT

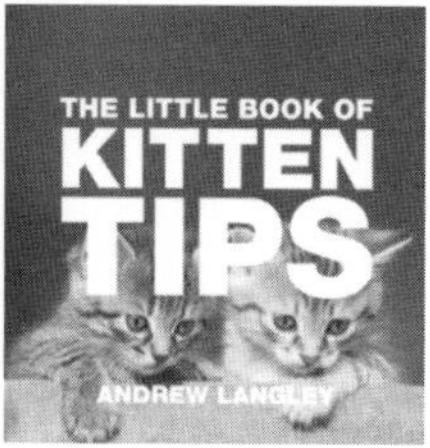
THE LITTLE BOOK OF
KITTEN
TIPS
ANDREW LANGLEY

MARMITE
PAUL HARTLEY
THE LITTLE BOOK OF
MARMITE
TIPS

THE LITTLE BOOK OF
PUPPY
TIPS
ANDREW LANGLEY

THE LITTLE BOOK OF
WHISKY
TIPS
ANDREW LANGLEY

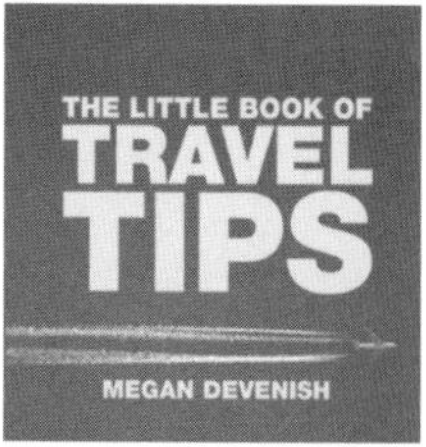
THE LITTLE BOOK OF
TRAVEL
TIPS
MEGAN DEVENISH

Little Books of Tips from Absolute Press

Aga Tips
Aga Tips 2
Aga Tips 3
Allotment Tips
Backgammon Tips
Barbecue Tips
Beer Tips
Biscuit Tips
Bread Tips
Bridge Tips
Cake Baking Tips
Cake Decorating Tips
Cheese Tips
Chefs' Tips
Chess Tips
Chocolate Tips
Christmas Aga Tips
Chutney and Pickle Tips
Cleaning Tips
Cocktail Tips
Coffee Tips
Cupcake Tips
Curry Tips
Fishing Tips
Fly Fishing Tips
Frugal Tips
Gardening Tips
Golf Tips
Green Tips
Grow Your Own Tips
Herb Tips
Houseplant Tips
Ice Cream Tips
Jam Tips
Kitten Tips
Macaroon Tips
Marmite Tips
Olive Oil Tips
Pasta Tips
Poker Tips
Puppy Tips
Rayburn Tips
Seafood Tips
Spice Tips
Tea Tips
Toast Tips
Travel Tips
Whisky Tips
Wine Tips
Vinegar Tips

THE LITTLE BOOK OF AGA TIPS

'Full of winning ideas for Aga owners.'
The Times

'Aga Tips is splendid! The best tip is about warming immovable jam jar lids – brilliant!'
Marjorie Dunkels, Aga owner